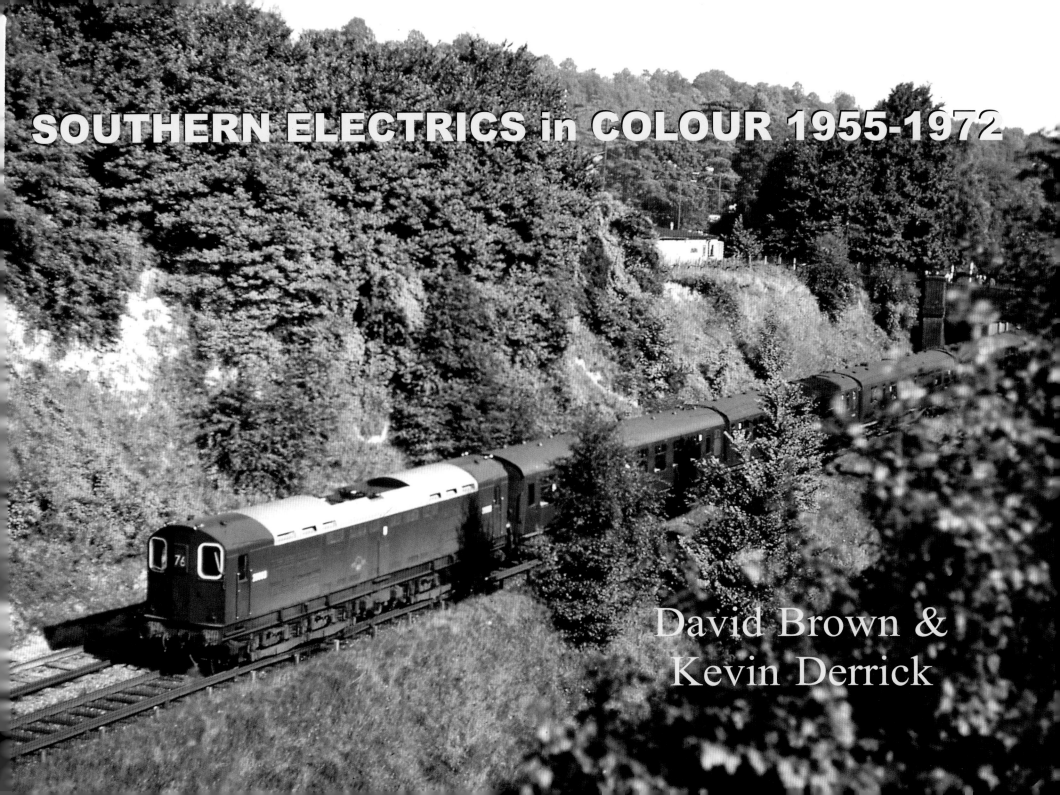

SOUTHERN ELECTRICS in COLOUR 1955-1972

David Brown &
Kevin Derrick

First published 2020
ISBN 978-1-913390-99-0

© David Brown / Strathwood Publishing 2020
Published by Strathwood, Unit 4 Shuttleworth Road, Elm Farm Industrial Estate, Bedford, MK41 0EP
Tel 01463 234004 - www.strathwood.co.uk

Cover: The most famous Southern electric train was undoubtedly the 'Brighton Belle' all-Pullman service between Victoria and Brighton. In cracking low winter light which brings out the rich shades of the distinctive Pullman livery, 5-BEL 3053 decelerates through the northern Brighton suburbs at Preston Park leading the 11.00 down working on 8 December 1965. *Colour Rail*

Below: Unit 2090 leads an eight-coach formation of 2-BIL stock near Deepcut (between Farnborough and Brookwood) on 28 June 1957, forming a morning peak-hour Ascot - Waterloo service via Frimley Junction, Sturt Lane Junction and Woking. The 152 units of this class were built between 1935 and 1938 for use on main line stopping and semi-fast services on the Central and Western Section electrified routes and were very much 'maids of all work'. *Colour Rail*

Previous page: 20003, the third and last of the Southern's Co-Co 'booster' locomotives, passes Coulsdon on the Quarry line with the Victoria – Newhaven Harbour boat train conveying passengers for the Dieppe channel crossing on 17 September 1966. By then it had been painted plain dark green and gained roller-blind headcode boxes. While reliable and successful in service these locomotives, inevitably nicknamed 'Hornby's', were deemed surplus to requirements in the face of declining freight traffic. 20003 was withdrawn on 2 November 1968 and its classmates succumbed two months later. *Colour Rail*

Above: 2-HAL 2651 leaves Victoria leading a Maidstone East (front) and Gillingham service, dividing at Swanley, on a sunny day in April 1955. The strong light brings out the early B.R. green livery to perfection. The first seventy-six 2-HALs were ordered for the electrification of the Maidstone and Gillingham lines, on which services commenced in July 1939. At left, passengers are boarding a boat train, including an ancient Pullman Car, at Platform 8. *Chris Wilson Collection*

An unidentified S.R.-type 4-EPB passes through pleasant suburban surroundings near Sydenham Hill with an Orpington - Victoria service on an unknown date in the 1950s. It is in as-built condition with the original 'cycling lion' emblem centrally on the motor coach sides. Aside from colour slide film and good quality cameras being awfully expensive in post-war 'austerity' Britain, we have to consider most photographers of the day who were experimenting with colour tended to concentrate their efforts and money of the steam scene. Earlier views such as this are therefore exceedingly rare. **Chris Wilson Collection**

Opposite: A pair of 2-HALs, led by 2632, stands at Horsham with an afternoon Three Bridges – Bognor Regis service on 7 August 1955. This service ran half-hourly calling at all stations down the Mid-Sussex line and connecting with the coastal expresses. Although mainly used on the Maidstone and Gillingham services until 1958, it was commonplace to see 2-HALs on Central and Western Section main line stopping services in place of 2-BILs. Their brutal interiors were, however, far less inviting. **Colour Rail**

4-COR 3106 reaches journey's end as it runs into Portsmouth Harbour with a fast service from Waterloo via Guildford in August 1955. The roof boards misleadingly read 'WATERLOO PORTSMOUTH ISLE OF WIGHT'. The 'one-eyed' appearance of these units, with only a single driver's lookout, clearly demonstrates why they quickly become known as 'Nelson stock' following their introduction in 1937. *Colour Rail*

2-BIL 2107 passes Ash Junction on 21 April 1956 leading a Waterloo – Guildford via Ascot service. The route to the left is the former direct line to Farnham via Tongham, which closed to passengers in July 1937 on electrification of the Alton line but was retained as a freight siding to serve Aldershot gas works. *Colour-Rail*

Opposite: A busy view inside Cannon Street on an unrecorded date in 1957, the lighting and shadows suggesting the evening rush hour On the right, 4-EPB 5258 has just pulled in but passengers are already boarding for the next outbound service before the motorman has changed ends and the headcode has been put up. On the left are pre-war SUBs 4330 (built 1925) and an unidentified Brighton-bodied example from the 4501-20 series. Although at this time the skeleton of the once magnificent overall roof was still in place, the Luftwaffe had removed the glass, forcing the construction of a few make do and mend platform canopies at the concourse end. *Colour Rail*

Another rake of four 2-BIL units, led by 2094, forms an Ascot – Waterloo via Woking service just west of Pirbright Junction on 30 May 1958. In this view the driving trailer composite is leading and the large windows on the corridor side, in typical Maunsell style, may be seen. The Sturt Lane Junction – Pirbright Junction section of the Basingstoke main line was electrified in 1939 as part of the Reading scheme, but only the local lines were equipped with conductor rails. This routeing was no longer possible following closure of the Frimley Junction – Sturt lane Junction curve in September 1964. *Colour Rail*

All-steel 4-SUB 4366, built in 1948, crosses the Thames and runs into Hampton Wick with a clockwise Kingston 'Roundabout' service via Earlsfield and Richmond on 31 May 1958. 4366 was one of the earlier units of its type and all seating was in compartments. The grab-handles around the cab windows and step-plates above the buffers enabled the motorman to change the headcode from the outside, as on these particular units the offside window didn't open. *Colour Rail*

Opposite: 2-BIL 2064 leads a 2-HAL and an all-steel 4-SUB into Haslemere with a morning Portsmouth & Southsea - Waterloo stopping service in September 1959. All suburban and semi-fast stock built up to 1950 could couple and work in multiple, and it was not uncommon to see a suburban unit as part of the consist of a stopping train to the coast. Wiser passengers would opt for the 2-BIL for the superior comfort and the availability of toilet facilities. *Colour Rail*

Above: 4-SUB 4340 was originally built as three-car unit 1510 for the 1925-26 Eastern Section suburban electrification and augmented to four coaches with one of the first all-steel 'six-a-side' trailers in 1945, by which time it could operate anywhere on the network. Here it is seen at Barnes on 20 June 1959, a year before withdrawal. Headcode 'inverted P' indicated a race special, probably from Waterloo to Ascot. *Rail Online*

Right: E5000 is parked in the downside berthing sidings at Dover Priory when new in 1959. This was the first of a fleet of twenty-four lightweight 2550hp Bo-Bo electric locomotives, classified Type HA, built at Doncaster for the two phases of the Kent Coast electrification. They were mainly intended for freight traffic, but also hauled the few locomotive-hauled passenger trains which remained, including the 'Golden Arrow' and 'Night Ferry'. *Colour Rail*

Type HA E5002 stands at Stewarts Lane, where a new shed was built to house and maintain these locomotives, in April 1959. Like the earlier Co-Co 'booster' locomotives 20001-3, they incorporated a motor-generator plus flywheel arrangement to cross gaps in the live rail without losing power and were fitted with pantographs as some freight sidings were equipped with simple overhead catenary. The viaduct in the background carries the South London line between Battersea Park and Wandsworth Road. *Colour Rail*

Newly outshopped following a repaint in the lighter shade of green also carried by the Kent Coast locomotives, Bulleid/Raworth Co-Co 'booster' locomotive 20002 is seen parked at Eastleigh on 9 May 1959. Cab front fittings include fold-down headcode discs incorporating electric marker lights, and an offside power jumper socket for use in depots. It is unlikely the light grey solebar remained clean for long. *Colour Rail*

Opposite: 4-SUB 4301 runs into Woking in September 1960 with what is believed to be a Waterloo - Esher (for Sandown Park) race special. As three-car unit 1297, it was built for the 1925 Western Section's Guildford and Dorking electrification, and was augmented to four cars with a new trailer in 1945. These units were shorter, and had a more pronounced point to the cab end, than the Eastern Section units shown on pages 12 and 17, but styling and passenger accommodation were otherwise identical. Note the 'School's 4-4-0 on a Basingstoke - Waterloo service on the left. *Colour Rail*

6-PAN 3028 leads a 6-PUL passing Norbury in the south London suburbs with a Victoria - Eastbourne/Ore service in about 1960. Seventeen 6-PANs were built for the 1935 Eastbourne line electrification, but they generally ran with a 6-PUL on coastal expresses via Haywards Heath until their demise in 1964-66. The pantry car, basically a corridor first with a small kitchenette at one end, is the third coach back. As catering vehicles they were soon found unsatisfactory, and the kitchens were unused through the 1950s. *Colour Rail*

1925 type 4-SUB 4352, formerly 1522 prior to augmentation, leads a Waterloo – Effingham Junction via Epsom service approaching Clapham Junction in July 1960. It was withdrawn on 25 November 1961, just over a month before the last of its class. With the end of the pre-war SUBs came also the disappearance of letter headcode stencils, which had originally been introduced by the L.S.W.R. in 1914. 'Six-a side' trailer 10353 survived to work in trailer set 900 from September 1963 and then in 4-SUB 4364. *Colour Rail*

Opposite: The twenty 6-PUL units were the first intended for express passenger service, being introduced for the Brighton line electrification of 1933. Here, 3004 departs from Worthing Central with a morning Littlehampton – Victoria fast service in about 1960. The PULs included a composite Pullman Car whose staff also served light refreshments to passengers in adjacent vehicles. The grounded coach body in the foreground served as offices for the builder's yard, many of whose supplies would have come in by rail. *Colour Rail*

4-COR 3110 draws through Clapham Junction nearing journey's end with a morning Portsmouth Harbour – Waterloo express on 2 July 1960. The continuous sideways oscillation of the end gangways gave rise to another nickname bestowed on these units by railwaymen and others – 'belly wobblers'. These gangways enabled all passengers to reach restaurant or buffet facilities but were quite an adventure to walk through – particularly for small boys, especially across complex pointwork at speed. *Colour Rail*

S.R.-type 4-EPB 5020 stands in the down centre road at Gravesend Central on 14 May 1960. By this time virtually all services on former S.E.R. suburban routes were being worked by this stock. Unit 5225 is in the down platform behind. Note the mixture of vehicles with and without cantrail-height rainstrips on both units; this mismatch was due to reformations following accidents. *Colour Rail*

A twelve-coach 4-COR + 4-RES + 4-COR formation, led by unit 3135, has just passed Farncombe station with a morning Waterloo – Portsmouth Harbour express, probably in the summer of 1960. Other than livery, the stock is in original condition with stencil headcode panel and whistle. Full restaurant facilities on Portsmouth expresses had by this time become uneconomic (it is doubtful whether they had ever been viable), and in 1964 the RES units were replaced by 4-BUF units transferred from the Bognor route. *Chris Wilson Collection*

Opposite: A second view of 20003, the final example of the Bulleid/Raworth Co-Co 'booster' electric locomotives and dating from 1948, shows it parked at Three Bridges in 1961 awaiting its next turn of duty. The main use of the class was haulage of heavy freight between major Central Section yards. 20003 differed from its earlier classmates, particularly in its cab design which clearly owed allegiance to contemporary 4-SUB electric units. As with 20002 pictured earlier, it was at this time in the same lined bright green livery as the E5000 class. *Colour Rail*

Charing Cross on 27 May 1961, demonstrating the take-over of all services by post-war stock. From left to right are 2-HAP 6023, 4-EPB 5258 and 4-EPB 5116, but unfortunately none is displaying a headcode so it is not possible to quote the services which they are operating. At this time two white blanks were shown on the roller blinds at the rear of a train and a red oil lamp was used as 'last vehicle' indication. On the far left, a six-car diesel-electric unit prepares to depart for Hastings via Tonbridge. *Colour Rail*

Above: This busy afternoon scene at the north end of Guildford station, repeated each hour through the off-peak period, dates from around 1961. On the right, 4-COR 3150 approaches Platform 2 leading a Waterloo – Portsmouth Harbour fast service. On the left, 2-HAL 2651 has just departed from Platform 3 at the rear of a stopping train from Portsmouth and Southsea to Waterloo and will call at all stations to Surbiton. Guildford Yard signal box is far left, with its unusual oriel window. *Chris Wilson Collection*

Opoosite: 2-BIL 2123 and a 2-HAL stand in the single electrified platform at Horsted Keynes, strangely the only one devoid of shelter, ready to form the next hourly service to Seaford via Haywards Heath and Lewes in about 1962. Preserved A1X 'Terrier' tank 'Stepney' in the background shows that the Bluebell Railway was in operation, providing some extra traffic for this otherwise very quiet line in rural East Sussex. Electrified in 1935 as part of the Eastbourne and Hastings scheme, it was closed in September 1963 under the Beeching regime. *Colour Rail*

26

Opposite: The 11.00 Victoria – Brighton non-stop 'Brighton Belle' all-Pullman service, led by 5-BEL unit 3053, speeds past Merstham on the Quarry Line (avoiding Redhill) in 1962. Apart from subtle changes to lining and other details with successive repaints, the distinctive Pullman livery remained unchanged from 1932 until 1968-69. Behind the train we can see some of the major engineering required for this cut-off line through the undulating Surrey countryside. *Colour Rail*

E6006 was the last of the six original Type JA electro-diesel locomotives, turned out from Eastleigh Carriage Works in 1962 and seen at Stewarts Lane when new. They incorporated a 600hp diesel engine to allow operation away from the live rail. There were detail differences between these locomotives; E6006 carries overall bright green with a grey stripe above the solebar but has no yellow warning panels and buffers are of the round 'oleo' type. The influence of the 5-BEL cab ends on the design is obvious. *Colour Rail*

A pair of 5-BEL units, again led by 3053, approaches Clayton tunnel (south of Hassocks) with the 11.00 down 'Brighton Belle' on 7 October 1962. Built by Metro Cammell in Birmingham, construction was all-steel, and the motor cars weighed a hefty and track-punishing 62 tons, by a small margin the heaviest in the Southern electric fleet. *Colour Rail*

2-HAL 2625 and an early 2-BIL from the 2001-10 series approach Ash with a Waterloo – Guildford via Ascot service on 15 June 1963. The prefabricated concrete footbridge in the background, made at Exmouth Junction concrete works, was of a type familiar over the entire Southern electric network.
Colour Rail

Above: This everyday scene from 1963 shows 4-SUB 4626 approaching Clapham Junction on the Windsor lines side with a mid-afternoon anticlockwise Kingston 'roundabout' service back to Waterloo via Richmond and Earlsfield. Dominating the near background is the overhead Clapham Junction 'A' signal box. The heavy additional roof, added during the war as air-raid blast protection, would partially collapse two years later. *Colour Rail*

Opposite: 2-BIL 2134 hums along between Havant and Bedhampton leading a Waterloo – Portsmouth and Southsea stopping service on 2 March 1963. 2134 was from the final batch of BILs, turned out in September 1938 for the forthcoming Reading line electrification, but from the start common user with the rest of the fleet. It was withdrawn in July 1970 and scrapped by Cashmore's at Newport. *Colour Rail*

5-BEL 3052 snakes through East Croydon leading the 11.00 down 'Brighton Belle' on 15 September 1963. The original Pullman crest has been replaced by an elongated version designed for the 'Blue Pullman' diesel trains and the 1960 East Coast cars. Riding was always notoriously lively, even after bogie modifications, and drink spillages, particularly when negotiating pointwork, were an everyday hazard. *Rail Online*

Left: 6-PAN 3035 passes Ditchling Common and heads towards Plumpton with an afternoon Victoria – Eastbourne/Ore service on an unrecorded date in about 1963. The handsome motor coaches of these units featured 'airstream' sliding glass ventilators rather than the large droplights of the PULs. The lack of through access between units was an operating drawback which would be remedied when the Portsmouth 4-COR stock was designed. *Colour Rail*

Below: The withdrawn motor coaches from 1925 4-SUB unit 4338 are seen stored in the S.R. carriage dump at Micheldever in July 1963 prior to being towed away for stripping and then scrapping. A draw for Southern electric enthusiasts and easily accessible on an 'at your own risk' basis, from the early 1960s onwards sidings here held electric vehicles which were withdrawn, stored or damaged. These two coaches were eventually broken up at Newhaven in December 1963, among the last to be dealt with there. *Mike Morant Collection*

Above: Bulleid's freakish 4-DD twins 4002 and 4001 stand at London Bridge with a morning peak Charing Cross – Dartford via Sidcup (avoiding Lewisham) service on 6 August 1964. These units were an attempt to squeeze more seats into a standard-length unit while keeping within the loading gauge, but for various reasons the concept failed. Clearly no-one has bothered to wash the cab front, which should be the same shade as the sides, for some time. It still retains the earlier style of roller blinds, which had larger numerals than subsequently used. *Colour Rail*

2-HAL 2655 has just arrived at Reigate with a service from London in 1964. The unit has divided from a Brighton stopping service at Redhill. This short section of the Redhill - Guildford cross-country line was electrified in 1932 as part of the Brighton scheme. *Colour Rail*

Opposite: Kent Coast Type HA 'booster' electric locomotive E5009 stands at Victoria platform 8 with the 11.00 'Golden Arrow' Pullman boat train to Dover Marine in August 1964. Onlookers mill around while a relief driver and his second man relax on a platform trolley awaiting their own train. Meanwhile the train crew are comfortable in their cab. *Colour Rail*

The second of the imposing Bulleid Co-Co 'booster' locomotives, 20002, stands in Eastleigh Works yard during an open day in July 1964. It is in its final mechanical form with the headcode disks and jumper cable socket removed, and roller-blind headcode panels added, but it did later gain yellow ends while remaining in green prior to withdrawal at the end of 1968. *Colour Rail*

The following three photographs were all taken from the A3 Battersea Rise road bridge across Clapham Cutting on 28 March 1965. In this view, 4-LAV 2940 accelerates away from the Clapham Junction stop with a Victoria - Brighton stopping service. The yellow cantrail stripes denote the peculiar arrangement of first-class compartments in these units from the early 1950s onwards, with two in the compartment trailer and five in the side-corridor trailer with toilets. In the background, a 4-SUB unit scuttles off towards Waterloo. *Colour Rail*

Although the 6-PUL units were built for the 1933 Brighton and Worthing electrification, by 1938 they had extended their sphere of operation to include express services to Eastbourne, Hastings and Littlehampton. 6-PUL 3013 heads down the Brighton main line through Clapham Cutting with a Victoria - Eastbourne/Ore express, not long before withdrawal. Only a few of these PUL units ever received yellow warning panels. *Colour Rail*

A slightly more head-on view shows 6-PUL (former 6-CIT) 3042, also passing Clapham Cutting with a down Eastbourne/Ore service. There was a composite trailer on either side of the Pullman Car so that all passengers could access first class accommodation when the Pullman was locked out of use and there was no through passage. *Colour Rail*

Running over the viaduct of the 1836 London and Greenwich Railway, S.R.-type 4-EPB 5010 draws to a halt at Deptford with a Charing Cross – Gravesend via Greenwich service on a crisp and clear day in December 1965. It is in typical mid-1960s condition and still carries a whistle above the motorman's lookout. *Chris Wilson Collection*

'3027' is the rear unit of the 10.00 Ore – Victoria service at Haywards Heath on 18 August 1965. Although numbered in the 6-PAN series, the original 3027 had been withdrawn the previous year and this unit was a short-term scratch rake formed entirely of former 6-PUL vehicles but without a Pullman Car, effectively making it a 6-COR. The particularly interesting 1964-66 period saw many unit reformations as on-train catering facilities were reorganised and the PUL and PAN units were steadily withdrawn. *Chris Wilson Collection*

4-COR 3106 runs through Haywards Heath with the 11.18 Brighton – Streatham Hill empty stock working, also on 18 August 1965. Comparison with earlier COR photographs shows that roller-blind headcode boxes and air horns have been fitted, while the livery is the second B.R. green with yellow first class cantrail stripes. Rectifier substations such as that on the right were a characteristic feature of the inter-war S.R. electrification schemes, as was the platform end warning signage. *Chris Wilson Collection*

Opposite: A 2-BIL & 2-HAL formation hums along through the beautiful Sussex countryside between Arundel and Amberley, with the River Arun in the foreground. This delightful image demonstrates how well the green Southern electric trains blended into the landscape.
Colour Rail

Right: A pair of 4-LAVs led by 2934 heads towards the coast south of Hassocks with yet another Victoria – Brighton semi-fast service in about 1965. The opening offside cab windscreen has been left slightly ajar to provide the motorman with additional ventilation on a hot day.
Alan Barber Collection

A side view of Driving Trailer Lavatory Composite S75382 from B.R. standard 2-HAP 6064 standing at Ramsgate on 13 July 1965. The HAPs were an E.P.-braked development of the HALs and were built in quantity, mainly for the Kent Coast lines. First class seating was squeezed into standard-width compartments, giving very limited leg room. The drab and uninspiring design was not very inviting, particularly when grubby. *Colour Rail*

Opposite: 4-CEP 7151 calls at Birchington-on-Sea with a Victoria – Ramsgate service on 11 July 1965 Clearly based on the pre-war COR stock but to B.R. standard design and with E.P. brakes, one hundred and eleven of the CEPs and twenty-two of the BEPs (with buffet car) were built between 1956 and 1962, mainly for the two phases of the Kent Coast electrification. There are clearly still enough staff at this point to tend the station garden. *Colour Rail*

Above: 4-CEP 7142 leads a twelve-coach CEP-BEP-CEP formation through Tonbridge with the 13.33 Ramsgate – Charing Cross service, fast from Ashford to Waterloo East, on 18 August 1965. The functional but uninspiring fronts of these units were simply standard Mark I coach ends with cab windscreens and headcode boxes added. *Chris Wilson Collection*

Opposite: A pair of 1939-type 2-HAL units, with 2602 leading, forms an afternoon Waterloo to Portsmouth and Southsea stopping service near Milford 27 June 1965. It is carrying the last B.R. green livery with a small yellow warning panel, a black triangle to show the luggage van position, and a cantrail yellow stripe to indicate the first-class accommodation. *Colour Rail*

Above: Approaching journey's end, 2-BIL unit 2121 leads a 2-HAL arriving at Lewes with a service from Seaford on a glorious summer day in 1966. Pictured from the foot of the signal box stairs, the non-electrified line curving sharply behind leads to Uckfield and the Oxted line. Five years later the BILs and HALs would have gone, the trains painted blue and the Uckfield line closed and lifted.
Graham T. V. Stace/Chris Wilson Collection

Opposite: 6-PUL 3041 stands at Ore with the R.C.T.S. 'PUL/PAN Farewell' rail tour on Sunday 24 April 1966. 3041 was originally one of three 6-CIT units with a higher proportion of first class for business trains but was reconfigured as a standard 6-PUL after World War Two. Following this tour, it was reformed as a 6-COR unit with the same unit number and survived into 1968, including a short spell in summer 1967 on Kent Coast services. *Colour Rail*

A side view of Pullman Composite Car 'Alice' in the formation of 6-PUL 3041 at Ore on the same date. Interior layout comprised, from the left, a kitchen and pantry, a two-bay first class saloon (eight armchairs), a first class 'coupe' compartment (four armchairs), a toilet and a second-class saloon (sixteen seats). Luxury indeed! Single Pullman Car operation had ceased on Brighton line expresses the previous Monday, but the 'Brighton Belle' would continue until April 1972. *Mike Morant Collection*

A final view of this rail tour shows unit 3041 at Eastbourne, next to one of the new 4-CIG units which replaced it. Like the 5-BELs, the motor coaches of the PUL units were of all-steel construction, rode very poorly and their weight was punishing to jointed track.
Chris Wilson Collection

Passing through typical sylvan West Surrey countryside near Camberley, a pair of 2-BIL units led by 2039 form a Waterloo – Guildford via Ascot service on 30 April 1966. The lack of a black triangle on the yellow patch indicates to platform staff that the luggage van at the far end of the unit. *Colour Rail*

A rake of three ex-works 4-TC trailer control units for the forthcoming Bournemouth electrification, with unit 423 directly behind the locomotive, are led into Clapham Yard by B.R.C.W. Type 3 (KA, later Class 33) D6506. The unpowered TCs were converted at York from existing Mark I hauled stock, some of which was already fifteen years old. Note that 423 is missing its trailer first. This was to allow an eleven-coach rake to be made up for working with a locomotive at the London end which would fit the platforms at Waterloo. In this 1966 view the locomotive is still in as-built external condition, as the S.R. was very late in applying yellow warning panels. *Chris Wilson Collection*

Following dieselisation of the Oxted line, a seven-coach formation of electrically-heated and air-braked stock was hastily formed up in September 1963 from spare EMU vehicles, specifically for certain rush-hour services which loaded heavily. Numbered 900, The end vehicles were from 2-BIL 2006 to provide limited toilet facilities and a brake van, while the others were Bulleid 'six-a-side' compartment trailers, one of which included first class seating. Hauled by a D65xx locomotive, it is seen leaving London Bridge with the 17.20 to Tunbridge Wells West via Edenbridge Town on 13 May 1966, with the former BIL motor brake second bringing up the rear. The pipework modifications required to allow the locomotive to provide braking, heating and lighting are clearly visible on the cab end. *Colour Rail*

E6036 was one of thirty-seven production electro-diesels, classified Type JB and later class 73/1, built at Newton-le-Willows in 1966. Differing only in detail from E6001-6, they were intended for freight, parcels and miscellaneous duties on the Bournemouth line and elsewhere and were electrically equivalent to a 4-REP motor coach. E6036 was delivered in overall B.R. blue with the new 'double arrow' symbol and is seen here in Clapham Yard having clearly not been in traffic for long. *Chris Wilson Collection*

The last new units to be delivered in the time-honoured green livery were the first of the 4-CIG and 4-BIG classes, the 'Brighton replacement' stock introduced between 1964 and 1966. These were the first S.R. electric units with a single intermediate motor coach and were also the only ones to have green livery with yellow warning panels from new. Displaying this smart colour scheme, 7322 leads a 4-CIG + 4-BIG + 4-CIG formation just south of Hassocks with the 09.00 Victoria – Brighton non-stop service on 17 September 1966. Note that the carriage roundel is on the side of the motor coach, an intermediate vehicle, and is not exactly central due to the location of a door. The many lineside photographers were waiting for a steam special; on such occasions it was common practice to take a test shot or use up the end of a film on a 'boring' electric train, otherwise pictures such as this would not exist. Fortunately, attitudes have changed with time. *Chris Wilson Collection*

BR Standard 4-EPB 5366 speeds though Berrylands with an afternoon Waterloo – Guildford via Cobham service, non-stop to Surbiton, on an unrecorded date in 1966. This unit was only four years old at the time and was one of the last to be built at Eastleigh Carriage Works which closed in 1963. The final fourteen of this class, including 5366, had a revised style of bodywork with improved window frames, tapered cab windscreens and shallow headcode panels. *Chris Wilson Collection*

Above: 4-COR units 3146 and 3116 slow for the Woking stop with an afternoon Waterloo – Portsmouth Harbour express in August 1966. The unit is in typical mid-1960s condition with a roller-blind headcode box and small yellow warning panels on the gangways. Behind, shunter D2041 awaits its next turn of duty in the down yard. **Chris Wilson Collection**

Left: 2-BIL 2107 leads three 2-HAL units approaching Clapham Junction with a Waterloo – Alton/Portsmouth stopping service, first stop Surbiton and dividing at Woking, in June 1966. Following its partial collapse, the wartime blast-protection roof has now been removed from Clapham Junction 'A' box, but the supporting framework remains. **Colour Rail**

A pair of 2-BILs, with 2065 leading, passes Woking Junction and heads towards Brookwood with the Alton portion of a stopping service from Waterloo on 17 August 1966. The concrete frame behind the train carries the external switchgear for Woking electrical substation. *Colour Rail*

Opposite: 4-SUB 4721 clatters into Clapham Junction with a Victoria - Coulsdon North service in September 1966. Built in 1950, 4721 was one of the 'standard' all-steel 4-SUB units with three centre-gangway open coaches and a slightly older compartment trailer recovered from a withdrawn 'augmented' pre-war unit. The underframes and bogies of the new coaches were also recycled from pre-war stock. To save costs, the Southern was adept at re-using serviceable parts from redundant vehicles to create 'new' electric units.
Frank Hornby/Colour Rail

Following withdrawal from capital stock in June 1960, the motor coaches of 1925 unit 4342 became an internal-user tractor unit within the confines of Durnsford Road depot, and are seen here on 18 August 1966 moving some wagons. The unit became redundant in 1969 and was broken-up on site the following year. 4-SUB and 2-BIL units await their next turn of duty in adjacent sidings. In the middle distance is the site of the recently demolished L.S.W.R. power station, and buildings on the skyline include the Airfix factory churning out their well-known plastic kits. *Colour Rail*

Below: Taking the Redhill line, 4-LAV 2938 passes the suburban terminus at Coulsdon North and slows to call at Coulsdon South with a Victoria - Brighton stopping service in April 1967. The signal box behind the unit controls Coulsdon North station throat and the adjacent Brighton line crossovers, while that in the background is at Smitham on the former S.E.R. branch from Purley to Tattenham Corner. *Chris Wilson Collection*

Left: One of the exclusive few Southern electric units outshopped in blue livery with small warning panels in 1966 was SR-type 4 EPB 5219, seen passing Clapham Junction with a Waterloo – Guildford via Cobham service on 4 February 1967. *Frank Hornby/Colour Rail*

Below: Propelled by a push-pull fitted B.R.C.W. Type 3 diesel (later class 33/1), 4-TC 417 pulls away from Wareham with a through Weymouth – Waterloo service on 22 April 1967, two months prior to the inauguration of the full electric timetable on the Bournemouth line. *Colour Rail*

2-BIL 2078 approaches Clapham Junction leading another BIL and a post-war all-steel 2-HAL with a Victoria – Bognor Regis service via Redhill and Horsham on 18 March 1967. The 'tin' HAL at the rear will be detached at Gatwick Airport (reversibly signalled Platform 2) and coupled to the front of the next up train after removing outgoing and loading incoming airline passengers' luggage. *Frank Hornby/Colour Rail*

4-REP 3003 stands in one of the centre sidings at the west end of Bournemouth station in about May 1967, probably following a test run. The two driving motor coaches were built new but the trailers, like the 4-TCs, were refurbished from existing stock. Each motor coach was rated at 1600hp, the equivalent of a JA or JB electro-diesel on electric power. In the steam shed opposite two rebuilt Bulleid Pacifics await their next duties, and a pair of diesel-mechanical shunters are also in attendance. *Colour Rail*

Opposite: New 4-VEP unit 7715 slows for the Micheldever stop with a Waterloo – Bournemouth stopping service on 17 June 1967, just three weeks prior to commencement of the new electric timetable. The first twenty 4-VEPs were built for the Bournemouth line but later batches replaced the LAV, BIL and HAL stock which feature prominently in this book. Although generally similar to the Brighton CIG and BIG stock, they had high-density seating and doors to each bay. To the staff they were known as '4 SUBs with corridors'. *Colour Rail*

Type JB electro-diesel E6041 stands in the down platform at Bournemouth, having propelled a train of TC stock from Waterloo on 30 June 1967. In the up platform rebuilt 'West Country' Pacific 34024 Tamar Valley waits to depart with a London train, including at least one coach in the new blue and grey livery. Full electric services on the Bournemouth line would commence on 10 July, after many steam drivers enjoyed their final fling with some spirited running in those final weeks. *Colour Rail*

The branch from Sittingbourne to Sheerness-on Sea was electrified in 1959 as part of Phase 1 of the Kent Coast electrification. Here, 2-HAP units 6110 and 6130 stand at Sheerness in about 1965. 6130 will shortly depart with a stopping service to Victoria, taking the Middle Junction – Western Junction spur onto the Thanet main line and avoiding Sittingbourne station. The bodywork and cabs of these units were to the B.R. standard suburban pattern, but they were geared to run at up to 90mph. *Colour Rail*

Opposite: An undated view in 1967 just as steam operation concluded that summer contrasts two types of Southern electric stock at Waterloo. On the left new Type JB electro-diesel E6024 awaits its next duty; note how a screw coupling has been attached over the dropped buckeye. On the right 4-COR 3162, whose oldest coach dates from 1932, older than many of the steam locomotives being withdrawn at this time, prepares to depart with a Portsmouth express. *Chris Wilson Collection*

Left: Seen from the concrete footbridge which spanned the line at this point, 4-LAV 2922 leads another Victoria – Brighton semi-fast train via Redhill passing South Croydon in August 1967. *Colour Rail*

Opposite: 4-TC 411 leads a 4-TC + 4-TC + 4-REP formation between Winchfield and Hook heading west down the Bournemouth main line in the spring of 1967, not long before the start of full electric services that July. Headcode 96 indicates a test or crew training working rather than a passenger service. The plume of smoke on the skyline indicates that a steam-hauled stopping train has just left Winchfield station. *Colour Rail*

Departing from East Croydon on 22 October 1967 with a Victoria – Brighton stopping service via the Quarry Line, 4-LAV 2924 clearly illustrates some characteristic features of the type. The 'pinched-in' cab and brake van, copied from contemporary S.R. steam stock, was not repeated on later electric units. The corridor side of the single lavatory composite trailer has large windows in typical Maunsell style, and the blank area makes it clear where the division between classes was located. Concrete bases for the overhead catenary masts used by A.C. electrics from 1925 until 1929 remain in situ on the top edge of the retaining wall. *Colour Rail*

This 1968 view south of Woking on the Portsmouth direct line shows a 4-COR + 4-BUF + 4-COR formation forming a Waterloo – Portsmouth Harbour semi-fast service. Leading unit 3121 was another 1966 early blue repaint with small warning panels and white unit numbers. The paint was applied by airless spray, giving a semi-gloss finish which soon weathered and faded badly, as clearly seen here. *Colour Rail*

Opposite: E6102 was the second of ten larger, 2550hp, electro-diesels of Type HB (later Class 74) provided for the Bournemouth electrification. They were thorough rebuilds of existing Type HA straight electric locomotives, conversion work taking place at Crewe during 1967. Largely due to their complex solid-state electrical control system, they were never very reliable and had a short working life of less than ten years. E6102 is seen here outside Crewe Works before heading south. *Strathwood Library Collection*

Above: 2011 was the first production 2-BIL (following prototypes 2001-10) and was constructed in 1936 for the Portsmouth and Alton electrification. Still in green but with full yellow ends recently applied, it is seen in 1968 taking the Quarry line at Coulsdon North with a Victoria – Bognor Regis service. The all-steel 2-HAL at the rear of the formation will be detached at Gatwick. The long concrete footbridge at this location, spanning both the station and the main line, was a favourite haunt of photographers. *Chris Wilson Collection*

Opposite: In the early days of the Bournemouth electrification, 4-REP 3006 passes Totton leading a Weymouth - Waterloo express. The REP will have started from Bournemouth, having picked up one or two 4-TC trailer units which were diesel-propelled from Weymouth. Smart enough when new and clean, as stated previously the 'eggshell' blue livery weathered badly and repaints of REP and TC stock into blue and grey with full yellow ends started in January 1968.
Chris Wilson Collection

Right: 4-LAV 2925 emerges from Merstham tunnel on the Redhill line with a southbound stopping service to Brighton on 28 April 1968. This unit has not yet gained air horns above the cab. The row of three box ventilators above the van were to cool the Metropolitan-Vickers electro-magnetic control system with which the LAVs, and other pre-1936 electric units, were equipped.
Colour Rail

Standard 'saloon' 4-SUB 4675, in blue but with a not particularly clean yellow end, arrives at Coulsdon North with a morning peak service from Victoria in 1968. Coulsdon North was the terminating point for suburban services calling at the intermediate stations at the London end of the Brighton main line. Between 1925 and 1929 the route was electrified on the 6700V 25Hz A.C. overhead system adopted by the L.B.S.C.R. but abandoned by the Southern in favour of the cheaper and more robust third rail D.C. system. *Chris Wilson Collection*

2-BIL 2145 stands at Seaford, having arrived from Brighton on an unknown date in the summer of 1968. The long guard's and luggage van of BILs, HALs and LAVs was intended to carry newspapers and general merchandise but did limit passenger capacity, particularly on eight, ten or twelve-car peak services. The BILs eked out their final days on coastal services such as this, ending in July 1971. *Colour Rail*

Opposite: The following three views are from the Dyke Road Drive overbridge, a fairly short (but uphill) walk from Brighton station. Looking north, 5-BEL 3051 accelerates away as the rear unit of the 13.45 'Brighton Belle' service to Victoria on 29 April 1968. The crest on the cab front has now been obliterated by the obligatory yellow warning panel, which clashes somewhat with the cream of the Pullman livery. The van train on the right includes vehicles of Southern, L.M.S. and B.R. origin. *Chris Wilson Collection*

Right: Among the items of modern equipment installed in Southern Electric maintenance depots were automatic carriage washers. 4-COR 3167 passes through the washer at Lovers Walk (Brighton) on 23 June 1968. They were clearly not so good at cleaning driving ends, which had numerous nooks and crannies to collect dirt. Behind is the recently closed Pullman works at Preston Park, with examples of 2-HAL and 4-VEP in the adjacent berthing sidings. *Colour Rail*

Opposite: Looking over the opposite parapet, 4-LAV 2923 departs from Brighton leading a Victoria stopping service, also on 23 June 1968. Visible in Lovers Walk shed and sidings are 4-SUB, 4-COR and 2-HAP stock, whilst shunting activity is taking place in Brighton lower goods yard opposite. 2923 belonged to that exclusive group of six 4-LAV units which remained in traffic until February 1969, although not officially withdrawn until April. *Colour Rail*

Above: 4-LAV 2924 passes Brockley leading an afternoon London Bridge – Brighton stopping service on 23 August 1968. It is travelling along the route of the London and Croydon Railway, opened in 1839 and very briefly served by atmospheric trains in 1847. The 'Catford loop' line from Peckham Rye to Shortlands passes overhead between Nunhead and Crofton Park stations. 2924 was another of the six 4-LAVs to survive into 1969. *Colour Rail*

4-COR 3166 passes Wimbledon with a Waterloo – Portsmouth Harbour semi-fast service in about 1968. Like 3162 and 3167 (above), this was one of ten additional units formed in 1965-66 from spare motor coaches and former 6- PUL and 6-PAN trailers, which could easily be identified by the ventilator bonnets over the door droplights. A 4-SUB is passing in the opposite direction. The Worple Road footbridge was another popular spot for photographers. *Chris Wilson Collection*

Running light, Type HA 'booster' electric locomotive E5011 looks rather lost in its surroundings as it passes Folkestone Central on an unrecorded date in 1968, probably heading for Dover Town yard. There were at least four variations of small warning panel applied to this class, and some never received them before being painted blue or converted into Class 74 electro-diesels. *Colour Rail*

After thirty-seven years of almost continuous running up and down the London - Brighton main line, 4-LAV 2949 stands at the coastal terminus in February 1969, probably during its last week in traffic. Six units had been given a stay of execution into 1969 as three of their 4-VEP replacements had been diverted to the Bournemouth line to form 8-VAB unit 8001, which was an additional unit to make up for a shortage of 4-REPs. Not officially withdrawn until April, 2949 spent time at Lancing, Stewarts Lane and Polegate before being broken up at Ickles, Rotherham, in August 1969. *John Vaughan/Rail Photoprints*

Trains cross at Sittingbourne in July 1969 during the 'green to blue' livery changeover. On the left 4-CEP 7114, in blue/grey with full yellow ends, picks up custom with a Victoria bound train. On the right 4-EPB 5123, in the superseded green with small warning panels, runs in with a Cannon Street – Ramsgate summer extra. Whether the young gentleman is most excited by a train trip or a visit to the seaside is not clear but let us hope he didn't need a toilet before arriving! *Chris Davis/Rail Photoprints*

Ex-works in B.R. blue with full yellow ends, 4-BUF 3080 departs from Havant leading an afternoon Waterloo – Portsmouth Harbour semi-fast service in April 1969. These units were built for the 1938 Mid-Sussex electrification but were transferred to the Portsmouth line in January 1964. The buffet car, with its distinctive 'Moorish'-style interior, is the third vehicle back.
John H. Bird/www.Anistr.com

A trio of 2-BIL units departs from Walton on Thames with the 14.53 Waterloo – Alton stopping service on a muggy 16 August 1969. Leading unit 2143 is still in green livery with small warning panels, while 2138 and 2043 are blue with full yellow ends. These units would soon be displaced from this duty by new 4-VEP stock and mass withdrawals would commence. 2143 was taken out of service that month and scrapped by Armytage's at Sheepbridge the following November. *Chris Wilson Collection*

Opposite: In very travel-weary green livery which it retained until the end, 2-BIL 2114 stands at Waterloo in September 1970, having just arrived from Ascot and beyond. Reading line services were the swansong of BIL (and HAL) units into Waterloo, and they were replaced by 4-COR stock the following month. 2114 was withdrawn that November and was broken up at Newport. *Colour Rail*

Above: Condemned 2-BIL 2084 was sent to Norfolk to be broken up in December 1971. A. King Ltd were a scrap-metal dealer based in East Anglia and their yard at Wymondham was responsible for the demise of many life-expired Southern electric vehicles in the 1960s and early 1970s. The crane in the background will no doubt set to work on this unfortunate unit shortly! *Chris Wilson Collection*

Opposite: The day after the last of the class were withdrawn from passenger service, 4-COR units 3102 and 3143 stand at Dover Marine with the Southern Electric Group's 'Nelson Farewell' rail tour on Sunday 1 October 1972. On the way back through Kent to London the pair were logged at 86mph through Headcorn, 11mph faster than the officially permitted maximum. *Colour Rail*

Above: The 'Brighton Belle' ceased operation on 30 April 1972 and the three 5-BEL units were withdrawn. On 8 April the R.C.T.S. ran a 'Brighton Belle Commemorative' rail tour using unit 3053, seen here approaching Barnham on the South Coast. In 1968-69 the traditional Pullman livery had given way to this modified version of B.R. blue/grey. *John Vaughan/Rail Photoprints*

The 11.00 Victoria – Dover 'Golden Arrow' boat train with First Class Pullman Cars also bowed out in 1972, the final working taking place on 30 September. Type HA (now Class 71) electric locomotive E5013, specially cleaned and decked out with headboard and flags for the occasion, stands at Dover Marine after arrival with the last down run. *Chris Wilson Collection*